BALLOON ADVENTURES

A Service Business Practice Set
for
College Accounting

BALLOON ADVENTURES

A Service Business Practice Set

A Document Version Practice Set
for College Accounting
with Two Solution Sets

including
**Instructions for General Ledger Software,
Peachtree Accounting, QuickBooks, and Excel**

by
Patricia A. Bille
Highline Community College

HOUGHTON MIFFLIN COMPANY   BOSTON   NEW YORK

Credits

Senior Accounting Editor: Bonnie Binkert
Senior Development Editor: Chere Bemelmans
Editorial Associate: James R. Dimock
Manufacturing Manager: Florence Cadran
Senior Marketing Manager: Todd Berman

Developers Credit:

- General Ledger Software: Cascade Design
  http://www.cascadedesign.com
  Lead Developer: John Cristofano

- Software Content and Guidelines: Linda Burkell

Visit Houghton Mifflin College Division on the Web:
http://college.hmco.com

ISBN: 0-618-38167-8

456789-MA-08 07

Contents

Instructions

Introduction to Balloon Adventures

You will be working for Balloon Adventures, a sole proprietorship service business located in Sedona, Arizona. The business was started January 1 this year by John Joseph, an avid balloon pilot. He works full time as manager, pilot, publicist, and technician. The business has developed a customer following that has steadily grown, mostly due to word of mouth recommendations. The business currently has two full-time employees: Becky Cedegren is the office manager as well as chase van driver, Brian Osborn is a pilot and salesman, and you are the new bookkeeper and the chase van assistant.

The previous bookkeeper left abruptly on June 30. On July 1, you were hired part time to be the bookkeeper, as well as to perform clerical duties. During the interim period, Mr. Joseph issued checks and deposited monies as needed, keeping note of each transaction on memorandums so that you could make journal entries. You have been asked to maintain the following records:

- General Journal
- General Ledger
- Checkbook (Check and Deposit Register)
- Petty Cash Payments Record
- Payroll Register
- Work Sheet and Financial Statements

Documents and business papers that you will be analyzing include:

- Memoranda
- Cash Revenue Reports
- Checks
- Sales Invoices
- Statements
- Petty Cash Vouchers
- Bank Reconciliation

Balloon Adventures uses a one-month accounting period. The accounting records are kept on the accrual basis. Balloon Adventures has retail sales of hot air balloon rides for cash and on account. The books were closed last month on June 30. An 8.2 percent sales tax is applied to the retail sales. The Chart of Accounts and beginning balances are listed on pages 7–9 of this workbook.

Solving the Practice Set

The *Balloon Adventures* Practice Set covers a one-month accounting period enabling you to acquire experience in performing the entire accounting cycle. Your instructor will choose the beginning trial balance, either Trial Balance A or Trial Balance B.

The *Balloon Adventures* Practice Set may be solved manually using the Journals, Registers, Working Papers, Report Forms in the back of this workbook. Portions of the practice set may also be solved electronically using Houghton Mifflin General Ledger Software, Peachtree Accounting, QuickBooks, or Microsoft Excel. The CD provides all the background information necessary to process the transactions for the *Balloon Adventures* Practice Set. Each data set, GLS, Peachtree Accounting, or QuickBooks, contains the two versions of the practice set. Instructions for using the CD begin on page 11.

Check Figures

The check figures for both versions of the practice set are on page 10.

Journalizing

Journalize all transactions from the source documents. The source documents include memos, sales invoices, purchase invoices, petty cash vouchers, checks, cash revenue reports, statements from creditors, and incoming checks. The invoices are date stamped on the date received by the company and should be journalized as of that date. Always use the most recent date on the document as your recording date.

Read and analyze each document. Circle or highlight the amounts, the latest or recording date, terms, invoice number, and any information that would appear in the transaction or explanation. Note that several of the purchase orders and invoices show a delivery fee and sales tax. Initial the document to indicate that it has been journalized.

Posting

Post the journal entries to the general ledger.

Cash Receipts: Mr. Joseph compares the amount of all cash and checks received with the source documents, then personally deposits all money received in the bank. Assume that deposits are made on the same day that the revenue reports are recorded. Enter each deposit as an increase (add) in the Check and Deposit Register and keep an up-to-date balance. Journalize the amount shown in the revenue report as cash received and as an addition on the next line of the Check and Deposit Register.

Cash Payments: Enter the transactions involving cash payments as a decrease (subtract) in the Check and Deposit Register beginning with check number 1748, and keep an up-to-date balance. Journalize these transactions in the General Journal, debiting the appropriate general ledger account or accounts upon which the money was spent. When the transaction has been journalized, write the check number on the corresponding interoffice memorandum and initial it.

Petty Cash: Record petty cash vouchers in the Petty Cash Payments Record beginning with voucher number 119 on page 30. Determine the amount spent, and journalize the reimbursement to petty cash in the general journal. Then post the general journal entry.

Payroll: You will be responsible for preparing the payroll information and entering it into the following records:

Payroll Register: Complete, total, crossfoot, and rule.

General Journal:

- *Journalize the payroll* and the employer payroll tax expense entries. Debit Wages Expense for the total amount, credit each deduction payable, and credit the difference between Wages Expense (the gross) and the deductions to Wages Payable (the net). List the numbers of the payroll checks in the explanation lines of the general journal entry.
- *Journalize the employer payroll taxes* by debiting Payroll Tax Expense and crediting the payroll liability accounts that indicate what the employer has contributed.
- *Journalize the payment of the payroll.* The Payroll register starts with page 96.

Bank Statements and Reconciliation: You will be responsible for reconciling the checkbook with the bank statement information given to you. You are also to journalize the entries caused by the new information on the bank statement.

End of the Month

You will be responsible for preparing the end-of-the-month documents for Balloon Adventures. When directed to do so by a memo, you are to:

- Complete the bank reconciliation.
- Complete the work sheet.
- Prepare the financial statements
  (income statement, statement of owner's equity, and balance sheet).
- Journalize the adjusting and closing entries.
- Post the adjusting and closing entries.
- Prepare the post-closing trial balance.

Getting Started

The account balances for the general ledger accounts must be entered before you begin to record the July transactions. Your instructor will assign you either Version A OR Version B. The trial balance for Version A appears on page 8 and trial balance for Version B appears on page 9.

Since the Balloon Adventures books were closed last month on June 30, beginning balances, for both Version A and B, use the date July 1, 20--. Using the assigned trial balance, notice that the year 20--, appears in the first block; write July 1 below it. Write the word Balance in the Item space next to the date, place a check mark in the Posting Reference space, and write the balance at the far right either under Debit or Credit—whatever the balance.

Note: If you are using the GLS, Peachtree, or QuickBooks files from the CD, the balances have been entered for you. Use the current year (or year 2005).

Maintain each of the following records:

- General Journal, beginning with page 116
- General Ledger
- Checkbook, beginning with check number 1748
- Petty Cash Vouchers beginning with voucher number 119
- Petty Cash Payments Record, beginning with page 30
- Payroll Register, beginning with page 96

Chart of Accounts

111	Cash		311	J. Joseph, Capital
112	Change Fund		312	J. Joseph, Drawing
113	Petty Cash Fund		313	Income Summary
114	Accounts Receivable		411	Income from Tours
115	Prepaid Insurance		511	Wages Expense
120	Land		512	Payroll Tax Expense
121	Building		513	Advertising Expense
122	Accumulated Depreciation, Building		514	Fuel Expense
123	Balloons and Gondolas		515	Utilities Expense
124	Accumulated Depreciation, Balloons and Gondolas		516	Balloon Supplies Expense
125	Van		517	Office Supplies Expense
126	Accumulated Depreciation, Van		518	Insurance Expense
127	Office Equipment		519	Balloon Repair Expense
128	Accumulated Depreciation, Office Equipment		520	Depreciation Expense, Building
129	Balloon Accessories		521	Depreciation Expense, Balloons and Gondolas
130	Accumulated Depreciation, Balloon Accessories		522	Depreciation Expense, Van
211	Accounts Payable		523	Depreciation Expense, Office Equipment
212	Sales Tax Payable		524	Depreciation Expense, Balloon Accessories
213	Employees' Income Tax Payable		525	Interest Expense
214	FICA Tax Payable		526	Miscellaneous Expense
215	Employees' Medical Insurance Payable			
216	State Unemployment Tax Payable			
217	Federal Unemployment Tax Payable			
218	Wages Payable			
220	Mortgage Payable			

Balloon Adventures
Trial Balance A
July 1, 20--

ACCOUNT	DEBIT	CREDIT
Cash	65,340.00	
Change Fund	100.00	
Petty Cash Fund	150.00	
Accounts Receivable	12,330.00	
Land	89,576.00	
Building	220,400.00	
Accumulated Depreciation, Building		3,713.38
Balloons and Gondolas	180,000.00	
Accumulated Depreciation, Balloons and Gondolas		1,568.00
Van	18,560.00	
Accumulated Depreciation, Van		487.00
Office Equipment	7,836.23	
Accumulated Depreciation, Office Equipment		850.00
Balloon Accessories	890.60	
Accumulated Depreciation, Balloon Accessories		128.00
Accounts Payable		17,178.10
Sales Tax Payable		1,032.40
Employees' Income Tax Payable		1,308.00
FICA Tax Payable		1,640.00
Employees' Medical Insurance Payable		535.00
State Unemployment Tax Payable		192.05
Federal Unemployment Tax Payable		83.20
Mortgage Payable		252,059.00
J. Joseph, Capital		314,408.70
	595,182.83	595,182.83

Version B Beginning Balances

Balloon Adventures
Trial Balance B
July 1, 20--

ACCOUNT	DEBIT	CREDIT
Cash	65,340.00	
Change Fund	100.00	
Petty Cash Fund	150.00	
Accounts Receivable	12,330.00	
Land	79,179.00	
Building	220,200.00	
Accumulated Depreciation, Building		3,863.38
Balloons and Gondolas	180,000.00	
Accumulated Depreciation, Balloons and Gondolas		1,568.00
Van	18,560.00	
Accumulated Depreciation, Van		487.00
Office Equipment	7,686.23	
Accumulated Depreciation, Office Equipment		870.00
Balloon Accessories	890.60	
Accumulated Depreciation, Balloon Accessories		128.00
Accounts Payable		17,178.10
Sales Tax Payable		1,032.40
Employees' Income Tax Payable		1,308.00
FICA Tax Payable		1,640.00
Employees' Medical Insurance Payable		535.00
State Unemployment Tax Payable		192.05
Federal Unemployment Tax Payable		83.20
Mortgage Payable		252,087.00
J. Joseph, Capital		303,463.70
	584,435.83	584,435.83

Check Figures for Balloon Adventures

Version A		Version B
611,007.23	Preadjusted Trial Balance Totals	600,260.23
2,187.67	Adjustments Totals	2,609.67
612,980.23	Adjusted Trial Balance Totals	602,655.23
400.85	Net Income Net Loss	21.15
12,800.00	Total Revenue (Income Statement)	12,800.00
12,399.15	Total Expenses (Income Statement)	12,821.15
313,009.55	J. Joseph, Capital, July 31, 20--	301,642.55
590,061.70	Total Assets (Balance Sheet)	578,722.70
598,781.08	Post-Closing Trial Balance Totals	588,034.08

Using the CD-ROM

The *Balloon Adventures* Practice Set CD provides all the background information necessary to process the transactions for Balloon Adventures. With an easy-to-navigate interface, the CD gives you the assets created specifically for the *Balloon Adventures* Practice Set and includes the program and data for the Houghton Mifflin General Ledger Software (GLS Version 3.1), the program and data for Peachtree Accounting 2004 (Version 8), the data for QuickBooks (2003 or newer), and an Excel spreadsheet with the blank working papers and forms.

Minimum System Requirements

This is a Windows® only CD.
System: Microsoft Windows® 98se, ME, NT 4.0 (SP 6), 2000, XP
Processor: Pentium 300 MHz or better
128 MB free RAM
800 by 600 screen resolution
4X+ CD-ROM drive
Printer
Sound card optional

Installation Instructions

The *Balloon Adventures* Practice Set CD installation procedure places the Balloon Adventures folders on your hard drive with a shortcut to the program launcher from your Start Menu. It then installs the application you have selected.

1.   Insert the *Balloon Adventures* CD-ROM into your CD drive.

2.   If the installation program does not automatically start, choose **Run** from the Start menu, type **X:\setup.exe**, where X is the letter assigned to your CD drive, and click the **OK** button.

3.   The "Welcome" window pops up. Read the information and click on <u>N</u>ext.

4.   The "Components" window pops up. Select the application you wish to install by clicking on the circle next to it:

       If you select Peachtree Accounting or QuickBooks, you will be asked to select the data Versions you wish installed.

Click in the box by "Microsoft Excel Working Papers and Forms" to access the blank working papers and forms specifically designed for *Balloon Adventures*.

After you have made your selections, click on Next.

5. Follow the on-screen instructions to complete the installation of the Launcher and the Excel Working Papers.

6. Next, the application (GLS or Peachtree Complete Accounting) installation begins. The installation program will then lead you through the rest of the installation.

7. Accept the default path, by clicking on Next. *The default path is where you install the program on your hard drive. It may differ from the default path shown.* If you wish to use a different directory, type that location in the "Path" dialog box.

8. Click on Next. A scale shows what percentage of the data has been copied. All files have been copied to the hard drive of your computer when the scale is completed. The "Success" window displays.

9. Click on Finish. You are returned to the desktop in Windows. Note: when prompted, you might need to restart your computer.

10. Remove the CD from its drive.

The Launcher

1. From the Start menu, select the Programs menu, followed by the Houghton Mifflin folder. Select the *Balloon Adventures* folder.

2. Click the *Balloon Adventures* application you would like to open.

3. The appropriate application will open.

Technical Help and Support

For technical support, call Houghton Mifflin's Technical Support at 1-800-732-3223 between 9 a.m. and 5 p.m. ET, Monday through Friday.

Send email to support@hmco.com for online assistance.

Using General Ledger Software

GLS is a custom-designed, simplified general ledger system that accompanies Houghton Mifflin accounting texts. The GLS application ties directly to the *Balloon Adventures* Practice Set and provides the required journal, ledgers, and reports needed to solve the practice set.

To Run the General Ledger Software

1. From the Start menu, select the Programs menu, followed by the Houghton Mifflin folder. Select the *Balloon Adventures* folder.

2. Click on the *GLS for Balloon Adventures* icon.

3. The *Balloon Adventures* window opens. Click OK and the General Ledger Software opens to the main window.

GLS Main Window

The interface, or main window for GLS, can be divided into one left pane, and one or two right panes. The panes can be sized by moving the mouse over the dividing bars. When the cursor changes to an up/down arrow, click and drag to adjust the window sizes.

Left-side Tree

When an item is selected from the pane on the left-side tree of the GLS window, the corresponding window is displayed in the right-side pane. To view two right panes, use the pushpin. (Help can be displayed in its own separate window.)

Expand and contract the tree with the +/− box to the left of the row or the left/right arrow keys on the keyboard.

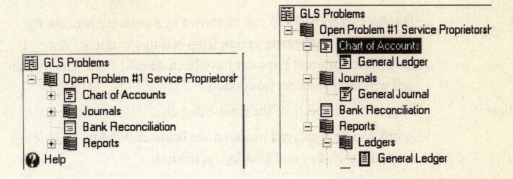

To toggle the visibility of the tree, or to hide it, select the **Menu** item on the toolbar, or **View**, **Left Pane** from the menu.

Main Menu Items

The main menu can be accessed by pressing the <Alt> key or by clicking on an item with the mouse.

File

Problem Reset	Reset the problem to its initial state, or before any user journal entries.
Printer Setup...	Open the standard Windows printer setup dialog box.
Export to Peachtree...	Select this option to save the beginning data for a problem in Peachtree format.
Quit	Ends to program. All work is automatically saved during your work session, so there is no save prompt.

Tools — Settings...

User Info	Name and Class can be entered. These will appear on the top of printed reports.
Options	Display the help toolbar in the help window. Display help in a separate browser window.
	Choose whether to display a default period on all reports or to be prompted for a customized period line on a report.

Repair	Select this option if the GLS application is noticeably slower or if the data appears to be corrupt. When the program is restarted, the database will be compacted and repaired.

View

Left Pane	Toggle the visibility of the left-side pane.
Toolbar	Toggle the visibility of the right-side pane.

Help

GLS Help	Display this help. Help can be shown in a separate window by selecting the appropriate option from settings window. *Note:* If the files for Internet Explorer have been deleted from your system you will need to select this option.
Main Toolbar	Toggle the visibility of the right-side pane.
	A link can be displayed in a separate browser window by holding down the shift-key and clicking on the link.

Toolbar

The toolbar (just below the Main Menu) keeps a history of which windows have been viewed in the right-side pane. Click on the small down arrows to view the history list. Select the **Back** and **Forward** buttons to move through the list. The **Menu** button toggles the visibility of the left-side pane. The visibility of this toolbar can be toggled by selecting **View, Toolbar** from the menu.

Grids

Grids provide a variety of ways to view data. All data entry windows and reports are configured as a grid.

To expand and contract a hierarchical grid, use the mouse to select the +/– box to the left of the row. To expand or contract all rows, select the +/– button above the grid.

Select any row by clicking on the row selection box at the right of the row. A right pointing triangle ▶ will indicate that the row is selected. Once a row is selected, data can be added, edited, or deleted. Click the **Delete** button to remove the row.

Most grids can be sorted by the information in a column. Click on the column heading to toggle between ascending and descending order.

Select the **pushpin** in the upper left corner to keep a window visible in the top right pane while additional windows are displayed in the lower pane. Panes can be resized.

 or   (selected)

Grid Navigation   To access the grid, click anywhere on it with the mouse. You can then use the keyboard to navigate around the grid. See the GLS Help for keyboard shortcuts.

Data Entry

Getting Started

If this is the first time you are using GLS, you will need to enter your name and class so they will appear on all printed reports. From the menu, select **Tools**, **Settings...**, then enter your name and class.

Opening a Problem

The list of problems, or practice set versions, is shown in the right panel. Select the problem by double-clicking on it, or clicking the Open button above the list.

Once a problem is opened, a list of relevant ledgers, journals, and reports needed to solve that problem will be displayed in the left pane for that problem.

Data entry can be performed in the Chart of Accounts, Journals, and Bank Reconciliation. Neither work sheets nor registers are in the General Ledger Software.

Select the appropriate option and enter the necessary data using the information in the transactions.

Chart of Accounts

The Chart of Accounts has up to three options from which to choose: General Ledger, Accounts Receivable, and Accounts Payable. For each practice set version, the Chart of Accounts already has been created for you. You may add and edit accounts, but you may not delete any account with a balance.

Select the Chart of Accounts from the left-side tree.

Adding an Account

Click the **Add** button. A window will appear that will allow you to enter information for the new account.

Type the name of the account. Select the **Account Category** and **Account Type**. Then click on the arrow ◄ ► buttons to scroll to the account number. When you click the Add button, the new account will be added to the Chart of Accounts for that problem.

Note: Each account name and number must be unique. Also, there can only be one account of certain types, such as Accounts Receivable or Accounts Payable.

Category:	Account Number range
Asset Accounts	100 - 199
Liability Accounts	200 - 299
Equity Accounts	300 - 399
Revenue Accounts	400 - 499
Expense Accounts	500 - 799
Customer Accounts	800 - 899
Supplier Accounts	900 - 999

Deleting an Account

Select the row with the account and click the delete key. If the account is in use or has any balance, you will not be able to delete it.

Editing an Account

To change an account name, double-click on the account name or select the row and click the Edit button. Enter any changes and click the Save button.

Note: Resetting the problem will return all accounts to their original status.

Journals

There are five different journals available in the GLS: General Journal, Sales Journal, Purchases Journal, Cash Receipts Journal, and Cash Payments Journal. Select the appropriate journal from the tree in the left pane. All data entry windows for the journals are configured as grids. For additional information about moving around a grid, see Grid Navigation.

Note: Only the journals required to complete a problem are available. Version A and Version B use only the General Journal.

General Journal

Select the **Add** button to add a new transaction. Enter the transaction date or select it from the list by clicking on the drop-down ▼ button. Type in the explanation. Enter the account or select it from the drop-down list. Enter the dollar amount in the appropriate column. Add lines to the transaction as necessary (a General Journal transaction must always have at least two line entries).

Select any row by clicking on the box at the right of the row. A right pointing triangle ▶ will indicate that the row is selected. Once a row is selected, data can be added, edited, or deleted.

To edit a transaction, select the row and make your changes. Click the **Delete** button to remove the row.

To **Print** a journal selection, click the Print button at the top of the window.

Sales, Purchases, Cash Receipts, and Cash Payments Journals

Select the **Add** button to add a new transaction. Enter the appropriate information to complete each row.

Select any row by clicking on the row selection box at the right of the row. Once a row is selected, data can be added, edited, or deleted.

Most journals (grids) can be sorted by the information in a column. Click on the column heading to toggle between ascending and descending order.

Posting

Transactions are posted individually by clicking on the **Post** button. The GLS will then automatically update the appropriate ledger accounts and balances.

Note: You may only edit or delete entries that have not been posted. If you discover mistakes after posting your information, highlight the particular line you wish to change and click the Unpost button.

Bank Reconciliation

1. Select **Bank Reconciliation** in the left-side pane.

2. Enter the Bank statement balance and the Cash balance per books.

3. Click on the Deposits & Checks tab. Click on either Add button to enter Deposits in Transit or Outstanding Checks.

4. Click on the Memos tab. Click on either Add button to enter Credit or Debit Memo information.

5. View the report by selecting Bank Reconciliation Report from the left-side pane.

Reports

The following reports are available in GLS:

Ledgers: General Ledger, Accounts Receivable Subsidiary Ledger, and the Accounts Payable Subsidiary Ledger

Trial Balance

Bank Reconciliation Report

Financial Statements: Income Statement, Statement of Owner's Equity, Balance Sheet (sole proprietorships); or Statement of Retained Earnings, Statement of Stockholders' Equity (corporations)

Subsidiary Schedules: Accounts Receivable Subsidiary Schedule, Accounts Payable Subsidiary Schedule

Note: Only the reports required to complete a problem are available.

The box at the top of the window will tell you how many pages are in the report. Move through the pages of the report by clicking on the ◄ ► buttons on the top of the report.

Printing a Report

To print a report click the **Print** button from the top of the report window. If you have selected to customize the report header (see Settings), a dialog box will appear and ask you to enter a Statement Date or an Accounting Period (two dates) for the report you want to print. All printed documents display your name, the problem number, your class (if specified), and the current date. This information can be changed in the Settings window.

Notes

*   Reports should be printed before closing entries are made.

- After closing entries are made, all the revenue and expense accounts have zero balances. A financial statement prepared from this data would show no revenues or expenses.

- The format of reports in the GLS may be different than the format shown in your textbook.

Problem Reset and Unpost

If you discover mistakes after posting your information, there are several ways to correct them.

Unpost   Highlight the particular line you wish to change in a journal and click the Unpost button.

Reset Problem   Select Reset Problem from the File menu to eliminate all the data entered in the problem.

Alternatively, you can correct the entry by:

1.   Debiting the account that was originally credited.

2.   Crediting the account that was originally debited.

3.   Recording and posting the correct entry.

Reversing the entry will eliminate its effects from all accounts.

Open Problems

The GLS comes with several open problems. Each open problem includes a default chart of accounts that you will need to complete. Then, if necessary, you will need to record a General Journal entry to get starting balances into the accounts.

The appropriate journals, ledgers, and financial statements are available for use in each type of open problem. The trial balance and bank reconciliation appear in each open problem.

Peachtree Conversion

Each GLS problem can be exported and then opened in the version of Peachtree distributed with this CD. Peachtree must be installed on your system before exporting a problem.

1. To export a problem, choose **File, Export to Peachtree...** Follow the on-screen instructions. The company files will be placed in the Peachtree directory.

2. Start Peachtree. From the opening window select **Open an existing company**.

3. Navigate to the folder with the title of your accounting book, such as Balloon Adventures. A list of all converted problems will be displayed. Select the problem you wish to open.

Note: If GLS is uninstalled, the exported companies will remain on your hard drive. To remove these, delete the *Balloon Adventures* folder under the Peachtree directory.

Uninstalling the GLS Program

There can be multiple titles using GLS, so uninstalling the program completely requires that each of the titles be removed first.

You can remove the *Balloon Adventures* program from your computer by following these steps:

1. Click on Start and navigate to the Control Panel.

2. Select Add/Remove Programs. In the Add/Remove Programs window, find *Balloon Adventures* on the list and click it.

3. Follow the on-screen instructions to remove the program. The UNINSTALL program will completely remove the *Balloon Adventures* files from your computer.

The General Ledger Software application itself will remain on your computer, but it will simply have no data in it. To remove the GLS program, follow these steps:

1. Click on Start and navigate to the Control Panel.

2. Select Add/Remove Programs. In the Add/Remove Programs window, find General Ledger Software in the list and click it.

3. Follow the on-screen instructions to remove the program. The UNINSTALL program will completely remove the General Ledger Software program from your computer.

Using the Excel Spreadsheet

The Microsoft Excel spreadsheet in the *Balloon Adventures* folder ties directly to *Balloon Adventures*. It contains the blank working papers and forms that appear in the back of the student workbook.

A spreadsheet (or worksheet or template) is a grid with rows and columns. The columns are denoted by letters and the rows by numbers. Any intersection of a row and a column results in a location with a unique address, called a cell. Excel allows for mathematical calculations among these cells. Tables can be built using cells containing numbers or formulas that relate to the other cells.

Basic Excel options or commands are used in the spreadsheets. Some general instructions are included below. See the documentation for Excel if you need additional help.

Many of the selections or commands on the menus have equivalent toolbar buttons. You may use either the menu selections or the button, depending on your preference.

Opening the File

Microsoft Excel, or an application that opens Excel files, must be installed on your computer. Launch the application and then:

1. Choose File, then Open.

2. Navigate to the *Balloon Adventures* folder on your hard drive.

3. Select the file with the name "Balloon Adventures.xls."

4. Click "Open."

The *Balloon Adventures* file contains 12 sheets:

General Journal	Income Statement
General Ledger	Statement of Owner's Equity
Check & Deposit Register	Balance Sheet
Petty Cash Payments Record	Post-Closing Trial Balance
Payroll Register	Bank Reconciliation
Work Sheet	Bank Form

Click on the tab at the bottom of the window to select the journal, register, working paper, or report form you wish to use.

| ◄ ◄ ► ►| \ **General Journal** ⟨ General Ledger ⟨ Check & Deposit Register ⟨ Petty Cash Payments Record |

Entering Data into a Spreadsheet

You will be entering data into specific cells in the spreadsheet. The other areas have been protected from any input errors you might make. Always press the <Enter> key after you have finished your entry into a cell. If you get a message box that says you are in a protected or locked cell (where no changes are permitted), this means that you are not in the proper cell. Move to the proper cell.

Note: Cells that you do not need to change have been locked or protected to prevent unnecessary changes. If you need to change locked cells, choose Tools, then Protection.

The print range and page breaks have been included in each sheet.

To enter a number, simply type it. Press the <Enter> key. You do not need to type a comma, or dollar or percent sign. The cells of the spreadsheets have already been set up with the appropriate number formats. If you encounter a cell filled with ######, this means that the number is too long for the cell.

To enter text into a cell, you begin typing. Excel will recognize by the first letter that it is text and not a formula.

If you make a mistake and need to erase the contents of a cell, highlight the cell and press <Backspace>.

The following table shows frequently used keys:

Key	Purpose
Esc	Cancels what you are doing. In edit mode, cancels the current entry in a cell.
Enter	Confirms selections.
Home	Returns you to the first cell in current row.
Page Up Page Down	Moves you to the top or bottom of the current window.
Tab	Moves to the next cell.
F1	Microsoft Excel Help contents.
=	Precedes equations and functions.
+ - * /	Indicates addition, subtraction, multiplication, division.

Cell Referencing

A cell reference or address is used to refer to the value in a cell. When one value is changed, all cells that reference that value are automatically updated. Cell referencing is done by simply entering a plus sign, then moving to the cell you wish to use somewhere else (reference) and pressing <Enter>. If you know the address of the cell you wish to reference, just type it after the plus sign.

There is another fast way to locate a value for cell referencing. In the cell type "+." Immediately, move to the cell to be referenced, using either the arrow keys or the mouse and scroll bars. You will notice a dotted line or moving border around the cell. Simply press the <Enter> key. You are returned to the original cell and the value automatically appears.

You may use any of the signs "=", "+", or "–" to begin a cell reference. If you do not enter one of these signs first, what you type appears as text in a cell.

You may refer to any cell within a sheet or to another sheet within the same file.

Copying the Contents of a Cell

You may use the Copy command to copy a formula to other cells in the worksheet that also require that formula. Click on the cell to be copied. Select the Edit menu then Copy or click the Copy button on the toolbar. Then, click on the cell in which to enter the value. Select Edit, Paste. Excel adjusts the cell references for the new value automatically. You may also copy a formula from one cell to another. Click on the cell with the formula. Select Edit, Copy. Move to the new cell. Select Edit, Paste.

Absolute Reference

To copy the contents of a cell where you want to use the exact same cell address, you use what is called an *absolute reference*. Designate the common cell address by putting a dollar sign ($) before each coordinate of the cell location. Using an absolute reference in the first cell of the column will allow you to copy the cell contents without adjusting the references.

Autofill

AutoFill is a shortcut to copy something to more than one adjacent cell. When the cursor is on a cell there is a tiny square in the bottom right corner of that cell. This is the Fill handle. Click and drag the Fill handle (cursor turns to +) down the adjacent cells in a column or row. When you release the mouse button, the value appears in each cell. This same procedure can be used to copy numbers, labels, formulas, and cell formats from one range to another.

Note: Formatting of the cell will also be copied.

Formulas

When you point to a cell, the contents of that cell are displayed in the "Formula Bar" below the toolbar.

To enter a formula, first type the "=" sign followed by the equation. Then press <Enter>. Use "+" and "−" to indicate addition and subtraction. The symbol for multiplication is "*" and the symbol for division is "/" in Excel. You may use cell referencing within the equation.

When you begin a formula with an "=" sign or use "+" or "−" when referencing a cell, Excel assumes that you would like the formula solved, and it will do so.

Functions

A function is a special built-in formula for performing certain frequently used operations. Within a function, a comma (,) is used to separate individual values. A colon (:) is used to include a range of values from adjacent cells.

The **=SUM** function is a short way to add a column of numbers. To use the sum function, type "=SUM" followed by the desired range within parentheses. To select the desired range, either type the first cell reference in the range you are adding or move the cursor to it. Press **"."** (period) to anchor this cell as your first cell. Then either type the cell reference of the last cell in the range or move the cursor to the desired cell and press the period again. Close the range with the **")."** Press the <Enter> key and Excel will execute this summing function. If the Σ button is visible, click on it. The function is automatically inserted. You only need to enter the range.

ROUND(*value, number of digits*) is the rounding function. The absolute value function ABS(*number*) gives the positive value of the number within the parentheses.

Special Formatting

As you work on a spreadsheet, you may wish to freeze the column or row headings. To change the setting, move the cursor into the top left cell of the area to freeze. Select Windows, Freeze Panes. This will freeze all cells above and to the left of the cursor, allowing you to move anywhere on the worksheet and still have column and row headings visible. Select Window Unfreeze Panes to remove freezing.

Saving Your Work

After you have completed your work, save your file to your hard drive.

1. Choose File, then Save As.

2. Select a folder on your hard drive.

3. Accept the file name in the File Name dialog box.

4. Click "OK" or "Save".

Printing Your Work

You might need to adjust the margins, page orientation, scaling, or font before printing. Change font or font size in the Font dialog box on the formatting toolbar. Select Page Setup and then the Margins or Page panel. Select the Fit To option to reduce your data so that it fits on the number of pages you specify, such as 1 page wide by 1 page tall. Select Landscape Orientation to print a wide worksheet.

Use the following instructions to print a worksheet.

1. Choose File, then Page Setup.

    Note: The Print button on the toolbar or Print on the File pull-down menu will send your work immediately to the printer using previous settings.

2. Select the Sheet tab or panel.

3. The worksheets already have a print range saved for them. The print range should appear in the dialog box. The print range may be changed by typing the cell addresses of the top left and bottom right corners of the range in a format like the print range presented for each file.

4. Click on the Print button.

Note: Depending on your computer setup, the instructions for printing may vary.

Using Peachtree Accounting with Balloon Adventures

Peachtree Complete Accounting and the *Balloon Adventures* data must be installed on your hard drive first.

The *Balloon Adventures* Practice Set provides two sets of opening trial balances: Version A and Version B. Included on the CD-ROM are two data sets, Version A and Version B, which contain the background information necessary to process the transactions for the *Balloon Adventures* Practice Set in Peachtree Accounting.

Opening the File

To open a company record:

1.   Enter the Peachtree Accounting program.

2.   At the Peachtree Accounting Startup Screen window, choose Open an existing company.

3.   At the Open an Existing Company window, click the Browse button. Navigate to the Program folder, followed by the Houghton Mifflin folder. Select the *Balloon Adventures* folder and then Peachtree.

4.   The *Balloon Adventures* Versions you have installed will appear in the left window.

5.   Highlight the company name and click OK.

Customizing the Company Name

The company name Balloon Adventures (A) or (B) appears in the title bar of Peachtree and will appear on all printed reports. If many students are using a computer lab, it's advisable to put your name in the name of the company title, which will then appear on all reports when they are printed. In addition, the company name can be changed to indicate it is the solution company record, and not the starter company record.

To change the company name:

1. Pull down the Maintain menu.

2. Choose Company Information.

3. In the Company Name field, change the company name to Student Name Balloon Adventures A Solution. (You may need to abbreviate the name to fit it all in.)

4. Choose OK.

The company name is now changed. When the company is reopened, the name Student Name Balloon Adventures A Version Solution will appear in the Open Company window and in the title bar of Peachtree.

Using Peachtree Accounting

Peachtree Accounting is a computerized general ledger package that is similar to a manual accounting system. Transactions are recorded in windows similar to special journals:

Manual Accounting System	Peachtree Accounting
Sales Journal	Sales/Invoicing window
Cash Receipts Journal	Receipts window
Purchases Journal	Purchases/Receive Inventory window
Cash Payments Journal	Payments window
General Journal	General Journal Entry window
	Payroll Entry window

Balloon Adventures requires use of **only** the General Journal.

See the documentation for Peachtree Accounting or the "Help" feature within the Peachtree program for instructions on specific features and options within the program.

Using QuickBooks with Balloon Adventures

The *Balloon Adventures* Practice Set provides two sets of opening trial balances: Version A and Version B. Included on the CD-ROM are two QuickBooks Backup data files:

> Balloon Adventures (A).QBB
>
> Balloon Adventures (B).QBB

each of which contains the background information necessary to process the transactions for the *Balloon Adventures* Practice Set. The Practice Set CD-ROM can be used with QuickBooks version 2003 or newer.

Note: QuickBooks must already be installed on your computer in order to use the data. The QuickBooks application is *not* provided on the CD.

After you copy the data set onto the hard drive, do the practice work on the hard drive.

Getting Started

Follow these steps to restore the *Balloon Adventures* data:

1. Start QuickBooks. If the Welcome or QB Navigator window appears, close the window. If a company file automatically opens, just ignore it.

2. From the menu bar, click on File, and then select Restore. The Restore Company Backup window opens.

3. Click on Browse and navigate to the appropriate directory on drive C, to get the backup from C:\Program Files\HMCO\BalloonAdventures\QuickBooks

4. Highlight the name of the company, Balloon Adventures (A).QBB, and then click on Open. The information moves into the Restore Company Backup window.

5. Make sure the Restore To section displays the location on your hard drive where you wish your work to be saved. If not, click on Browse and navigate to the appropriate directory on drive C, and then click Save.

6. The "File name" box displays Balloon Adventures (A).QBW or Balloon Adventures (B).QBW. Click on Restore.

7. A screen pops up that says, "Your data has been restored successfully." Click on OK. The menu bar for Balloon Adventures - QuickBooks displays.

Using QuickBooks

See the documentation for QuickBooks or the "Help" feature within the QuickBooks program for instructions on specific features and options within the program.

Keep these things in mind if you use the QuickBooks data for Balloon Adventures:

Use QuickBooks 2003 (or newer) to record entries for *Balloon Adventures*.

The Practice Set CD includes two QuickBooks Backup data files for Balloon Adventures. You selected one of these files when you loaded the QuickBooks data from the Practice Set CD.

Balloon Adventures (A).QBB

Balloon Adventures (B).QBB

Balloon Adventures ending balances have been entered for June 2005. Be sure to select the correct period before you begin, July 2005.

QuickBooks automatically adds the following general ledger accounts as necessary:
Account No. 3900, Retained Earnings
Account No. 1499, Undeposited Funds
Account No. 4999, Uncategorized Income
Account No. 6999, Uncategorized Expenses
These accounts will not have balances or affect the operation of QuickBooks.

Because QuickBooks accomplishes many of its accounting tasks in the background, posting is automatic when you record transactions.

Record all entries for Balloon Adventures in the General Journal.

Remember to make regular backups of your QuickBooks files.

Business Papers

Balloon Adventures

Memorandum

To _____Bookkeeper_____

From _____J. Joseph_____   Date _July 1, 20--_

Issued check # 1748 to Marvin Realty in the amount of $1,140.00 for July mortgage payment.

Note: $285 is applied towards the principal (Mortgage Payable, acct. 220), and $855.00 is interest (Interest Expense, acct. 525).

Balloon Adventures

Memorandum

To _____Bookkeeper_____

From _____J. Joseph_____   Date _July 1, 20--_

Issued check # 1749 to the City of Sedona, in the amount of $75.00 for our business license renewal.

(Debit Miscellaneous Expense)

Balloon Adventures

Memorandum

To   *Bookkeeper*

From   *J. Joseph*   Date   *July 1, 20--*

Issued check # 1750 to Newkirk Auto Insurance for the 6-month van insurance policy in the amount of $600.

(Debit Prepaid Insurance)

Balloon Adventures

Memorandum

To   *Bookkeeper*

From   *J. Joseph*   Date   *July 1, 20--*

Issued check # 1751 to Shermantine Insurance Agency in the amount of $492.80 for quarterly fire, theft, and liability insurance.

(Debit Prepaid Insurance)

Balloon Adventures

Memorandum

To _____ *Bookkeeper* _____

From _____ *J. Joseph* _____   Date _____ *July 1, 20--* _____

FYI: The following is a list of customers who have ongoing accounts for balloon services. You will notice the beginning balance of Accounts Receivable in the General Ledger is $12,330.

The Tour Group	$ 980.00
Service Corporation International	525.00
The Wedding People	1,950.00
Desert Hotels	3,480.00
Yucca Tours	3,250.00
Red Rock Tours	1,750.00
Wild Life Tours	395.00
*Total	$12,330.00

*There is nothing to record; for your information only.

Balloon Adventures

Memorandum

To _____ *Bookkeeper* _____

From _____ *J. Joseph* _____   Date _____ *July 1, 20--* _____

Received payment of $1,950 from The Wedding People.

* I will handle posting to all the individual customer accounts.

Balloon Adventures

Memorandum

To   _Bookkeeper_

From   _J. Joseph_   Date _July 2, 20--_

Received payment of $3,480.00 on account from Desert Hotels.

Balloon Adventures

Memorandum

To   _Bookkeeper_

From   _J. Joseph_   Date _July 2, 20--_

Issued check # 1752, in the amount of $535.00, to Highline Medical Insurance for July premiums for employees' medical insurance.

Balloon Adventures
Memorandum

To   *Bookkeeper*

From   *J. Joseph*   Date   *July 3, 20- -*

Received payment of $980.00 on account from The Tour Group.

Balloon Adventures

Memorandum

To   *Bookkeeper*

From   *J. Joseph*   Date   *July 3, 20- -*

Purchased balloon supplies on account from Air Supplies, Inc.,
$218.45.

Remember to debit Balloon Supplies Expense.

Balloon Adventures

Cash Revenue Report

For Period _July 1-5, 20- -_   Date _July 6, 20- -_

Income from Tours Credit	Sales Tax Payable Credit	Net Cash Debit
$2,350.00	$192.70	$2,542.70

SCI
Service Corporation International
3627 West Seventh
Phoenix, AZ 85023

No. **9627**
11-946
1953

Rec'd 7/06

July 3, 20--

PAY TO THE
ORDER OF ___BALLOON ADVENTURES___ $ ___525.00___

Five Hundred Twenty Five and no cents ---------------------- DOLLARS

National Bank
3024 Highway 89A
Sedona, AZ 86336

FOR On account, in full

BY _Tammy L. Raymond_

|:1953||0946|023 04427936||9627

Yucca Tours
3602 Jordan Road
Scottsdale, AZ 85251

No. **5438**

$\underline{1\text{-}238}$
1953

Rec'd 7/07

July 5,   20--

PAY TO THE
ORDER OF _____ BALLOON ADVENTURES _____ $ _____ 3,250.00 _____

Three Thousand Two Hundred Fifty Dollars and 00/100 ------------- DOLLARS

Arizona Bank
4200 South Main
Scottsdale, AZ 85251

FOR Account paid in full.

Elizabeth Johnson

|:1953||0238|033 01420434||5438

Balloon Suppliers
3641 Uptown Road
Sedona, AZ 86336

Rec'd 7/08

Invoice No. 791

SALES INVOICE

Sold To   *Balloon Adventures*

Address   *15 Coffee Pot Road*

            Sedona, AZ 86336

Deliver To   *Same*

Address

Invoice Date 7/9/20--	Date Shipped 7/9/20--	Ship VIA Overland	Salesperson et	FOB Scottsdale	Terms 2/10, n30	Order No. Wholesale
Quantity	We Were Pleased To Supply The Items Listed Below				Price	Amount
3	Propane Tanks (20 gallons)				27.40	$82.20
					TOTAL	$82.20

Please debit Fuel Expense and credit Accounts Payable since we charged it.

Red Rock Tours
212 Uptown Road
Sedona, AZ 86336

Rec'd 7/08

No. **1722**

1-238
1953

July 6,   20--

PAY TO THE
ORDER OF   **BALLOON ADVENTURES** $ 1,750.00

One Thousand Seven Hundred Fifty Dollars and 00/100   DOLLARS

Arizona Bank
4200 South Main
Scottsdale, AZ 85251

FOR Account paid in full.

Gretta Raynor

|:1953||0238|098 017330602||1722

Sedona Stationers
2156 Basha's Way
Sedona, AZ 86336
(928) 555-3400

Rec'd 7/09

Invoice No. 3167
Date: 7/07/20--

Sold To   BALLOON ADVENTURES   **Deliver To**   Same
Address   15 Coffee Pot Road   **Address**
                Sedona, AZ 86336

Customer's Order	Items	Terms 2/10, n/30	VIA Fast Freight	Balance
1	Toner cartridge (Okidata OL810)-rebuilt		89.95	89.95
1 box	White, 20 lb. printer paper		26.00	26.00
			Subtotal	115.95
			Sales Tax	9.51
			Total	**$125.46**

Balloon Adventures

Memorandum

To   _Bookkeeper_

From _J. Joseph_   Date _July 9, 20--_

Issued check # 1753, in the amount of $288.00 to Menninger Chemical for supplies purchased on account in June.

Statement

Sedona Red Rock News

168 Schnebly Road
Sedona, AZ 86336
(928) 282-1000

Rec'd 7/10

Statement No. 3296

Sold To	BALLOON ADVENTURES	Date	7/10/20--
Address	15 Coffee Pot Road	Terms	2/10, n/30
	Sedona, AZ 86336	Enclosed $	247.00

Date	Charges and Credits	Balance
	Color Ad. ¼ page. Sunday/Wednesday	247.00

PLEASE PAY IN FULL.

Issued Check # 1754 in the amount of $247.00 to Sedona Red Rock News.

Wild Life Tours
87 Country Road
Sedona, AZ 86336

Rec'd 7/10

No. **7435**

1-831
1953

July 8, 20--

PAY TO THE
ORDER OF ___ **BALLOON ADVENTURES** ___ $ ___ 395.00 ___

Three Hundred Ninety-five Dollars and 00/100 -------------------- DOLLARS

Bank One
614 West 89A
Sedona, AZ 86336

FOR Account paid in full. ___

Celina Ross

|:1953||3831|011 04124034||7435

Balloon Adventures

Cash Revenue Report

For Period _July 6-12, 20--_   Date _July 13, 20--_

Income from Tours Credit	Sales Tax Payable Credit	Net Cash Debit
$1,550.00	$127.10	$1,677.10

Balloon Adventures
Memorandum

To   *Bookkeeper*

From   *J. Joseph*   ·   Date *July 13, 20--*

Issued check # 1755, in the amount of $2,948.00 to City Bank for the previous quarter's FICA Tax ($1,640.00) and Employees' Income Taxes ($1,308.00)--April, May, June--employee deductions for FICA Tax Payable and Employees' Income Tax Payable and employer's contribution for FICA Tax Payable.

Sales Invoice

Metz Balloon Tech
3246 Commerce Street
Phoenix, AZ 85020
(623) 463-5789

Rec'd 7/13

Invoice No.   H456983

Sold To	**BALLOON ADVENTURES**	Deliver To	same
Address	**15 Coffee Pot Road**	Address	
	Sedona, AZ 86336		

CUSTOMER'S ORDER K8765	TERMS 2/20, n/60	VIA Drake	DELIVERY 7/14/20--	AMOUNT
1	Super-Carry Gondola		4199.99	4199.99
			Shipping	79.02
			Sales Tax	350.88
			Total	$4,629.89

Petty Cash Voucher

Balloon Adventures

No. 119

Paid To: _John Joseph_

Account: _Office Supplies Expense_   Date _July 14, 20--_

For: _Film for the fax machine_   Amount $24.98

Balloon Adventures

Memorandum

To _Bookkeeper_

From _J. Joseph_   Date _July 14, 20--_

Issued check # 1756, in the amount of $1,032.40, to the State Department of Revenue for the sales tax we collected in June.

Balloon Adventures

Memorandum

To   *Bookkeeper*

From   *J. Joseph*   Date   *July 15, 20--*

1. *Compute the payroll below and then complete the payroll register.*

2. *Journalize the payroll and all employee and employer taxes covering the period of July 1 to 15—overtime does not apply since nobody has worked more than 40 hours in a week.*

Becky Cedergren (65 hours @ $21.00 per hour), Check # 1757

Gross amount (hours x rate)	
Federal income tax withheld (Married, 1 deduction)	202.00
Social Security tax withheld (taxable earnings x 0.062)	
Medicare tax withheld (taxable earnings x 0.0145)	
Medical insurance withheld ($40 on first check of month only)	
Net amount (calculate gross amount minus deductions)	

Brian Osborn (60 hours @ $19.50 per hour), Check # 1758

Gross amount (hours x rate)	
Federal income tax withheld (Married, 1 deduction)	150.00
Social Security tax withheld (taxable earnings x 0.062)	
Medicare tax withheld (taxable earnings x 0.0145)	
Medical insurance withheld ($40 on first check of month only)	
Net amount (calculate gross amount minus deductions)	

You (55 hours @ $14.50 per hour), Check # 1759

Gross amount (hours x rate)	
Federal income tax withheld (Married, 2 deductions)	72.00
Social Security tax withheld (taxable earnings x 0.062)	
Medicare tax withheld (taxable earnings x 0.0145)	
Medical insurance withheld ($40 on first check of month only)	
Net amount (calculate gross amount minus deductions)	

* *Note that the limit on Social Security is $84,900 and that there is no limit on Medicare.*

Balloon Adventures

Memorandum

To   *Bookkeeper*

From   *J. Joseph*   Date *July 15, 20--*

1.   Issued checks 1757 through 1759 for payroll period ending July 15, 20--.

2.   Journalize the State Unemployment Tax @ 5.4% of the taxable earnings for this payroll. *

3.   Journalize the Federal Unemployment Tax @ 0.8% of the taxable earnings for this payroll as well as the employer's portion of Federal Unemployment Tax. *

Note: Federal Unemployment and State Unemployment taxes apply only to the first $7,000 of earnings per year. See the payroll register for earnings taxed up to this payroll.

Balloon Adventures

Memorandum

To   *Bookkeeper*

From   *J. Joseph*   Date *July 15, 20--*

Issued check # 1760, in the amount of $800.00, for my personal use.

Balloon Adventures

Memorandum

To   _Bookkeeper_

From   _J. Joseph_   Date _July 15, 20- -_

Issued check # 1761, in the amount of $182.79, to the TentMakers for balloon repairs.

Balloon Adventures

Memorandum

To   _Bookkeeper_

From   _J. Joseph_   Date _July 15, 20- -_

Strohm Real Estate bought 10 Sunset Champagne Tours at $225 each and charged the cost of $2,250.00.

Northern Arizona Power Company   7320 Elm Street Scottsdale, AZ 85256

Rec'd 7/15

Billing Through: July 13, 20--
Customer: BALLOON ADVENTURES
                       15 Coffee Pot Road
                       Sedona, AZ 86336
                       4790042-52-C-95

CODE	METER NUMBER	READING PREVIOUS	READING PRESENT	MULTIPLIER	KILOAZTT HRS.	AMOUNT
7	8629427MF17	5728	6021	42	12,306	108.52
					PLEASE PAY	108.52

Issued check # 1762, in the amount of $108.52. JJ.
(Debit Utilities Expense).

PRICILA'S

Rec'd 7/16

Sold To   BALLOON ADVENTURES   **Deliver To**   Same
Address   15 Coffee Pot Road   **Address**
                 Sedona, AZ 86336

Customer's Order	Items	Terms 2/10, n/30		Balance
1	Floral Bouquet	46.00		46.00
	Sales Tax			3.77

Issued Check # 1763, in the amount of $49.77.
Inv. # J3601 for Moonlight Madness event   JJ

| | | | **Total** | 49.77 |

(Debit Miscellaneous Expense)

Sales Invoice

OFFICE MART

2632 Pinion Place
Scottsdale, AZ 85256
(623) 382-9356

Rec'd 7/16

Invoice No. 793

Sold To: _Balloon Adventures_   Deliver To: _Same_

Address: _15 Coffee Pot Road_   Address: _____

Sedona, AZ 86336

Invoice Date 7/14/20--	Date Shipped 7/14/20--	Ship VIA Will Call	Salesperson tr	FOB	Terms n/30	Order No.
Quantity					**Price**	**Amount**
1	Combination copier/fax/printer Model 8962				540.00	540.00
					Subtotal	540.00
					Tax	44.28
					TOTAL	584.28

Balloon Adventures

Memorandum

To _Bookkeeper_

From _J. Joseph_   Date _July 17, 20--_

Purchased blankets, goggles, and fire extinguishers, on account, from Brandmeier Equipment, $482.36. Terms 1/10, net 30. Debit Balloon Accessories.

Balloon Adventures

Memorandum

To _____Bookkeeper_____

From _____J. Joseph_____   Date _____July 17, 20--_____

Issued check # 1764, in the amount of $125.46, to Chase Office Supplies for items purchased on account last month.

Balloon Adventures

Cash Revenue Report

For Period _____July 13-19, 20--_____   Date _____July 20, 20--_____

Income from Tours Credit	Sales Tax Payable Credit	Net Cash Debit
$1,850.00	$151.70	$2,001.70

OFFICE MART

2632 Pinion Place
Scottsdale, AZ 85256
(623) 382-9356

Sales Invoice

Rec'd 7/20

Invoice No. 799

Sold To: *Balloon Adventures*

Address: *15 Coffee Pot Road*

Sedona, AZ 86336

Deliver To: *Same*

Address:

Invoice Date 7/17/20--	Date Shipped 7/17/20--	Ship VIA Will Call	Salesperson tr	FOB	Terms n/30	Order No.
Quantity					Price	Amount
2	Desk Pack (clips, bands, staple remover, tape, scissors)				24.85	49.90
1	Stapler				19.95	19.95
1	Time clock				49.95	49.95
					Subtotal	119.80
					Tax	9.80
					TOTAL	129.60

Balloon Adventures

Memorandum

To   *Bookkeeper*

From   *J. Joseph*

Date *July 21, 20--*

Issued check 1765, in the amount of $236.80, to Tasco Fuels for jeep fuel. (Debit Fuel Expense)

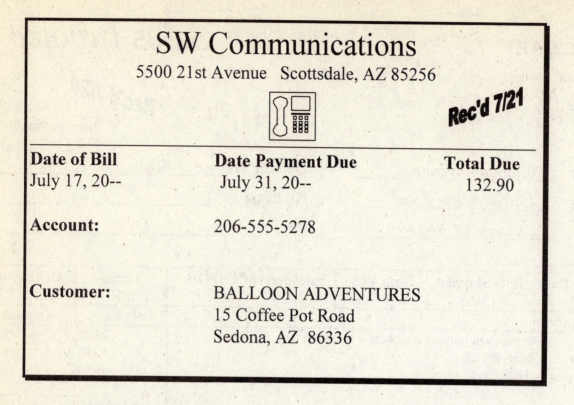

SW Communications

5500 21st Avenue   Scottsdale, AZ 85256

Rec'd 7/21

Date of Bill	**Date Payment Due**	**Total Due**
July 17, 20--	July 31, 20--	132.90

Account: 206-555-5278

Customer: BALLOON ADVENTURES
15 Coffee Pot Road
Sedona, AZ 86336

(Debit Utilities Expense, credit Accounts Payable).

Petty Cash Voucher

Balloon Adventures

No. 120

Paid To: *John Joseph*

Account: *Miscellaneous Expense*   Date *July 22, 20--*

For: *U. S. Postal Stamps*   *Amount $22.20*

Sedona Printing
2589 Highway 89A
Sedona, AZ 86336
(928) 282-35400

Rec'd 7/22

Invoice No. 217
Date 7/19/20--

Sold To: BALLOON ADVENTURES

Address: 15 Coffee Pot Road
Sedona, AZ 86336

Deliver To: Same

Quantity Ordered	Items	Terms 2/10, n/30	Delivery Date	8/19/20--
500	Brochure 1			75.00
			Subtotal	75.00
			Sales Tax	6.15
		Total		$81.15

Due upon receipt of order

(Debit Advertising Expense)

Balloon Adventures

Memorandum

To _Bookkeeper_

From _J. Joseph_

Date _July 23, 20--_

Issued check 1766, in the amount of $900.00, to Oak Tree Furniture for office furniture we purchased May 28. The terms were 60 days same as cash.

Balloon Adventures
Memorandum

To   _Bookkeeper_

From   _J. Joseph_   Date _July 24, 20--_

Issued check # 1767, in the amount of $37.50, to Charge-All for recharging the fire extinguishers. (Debit Miscellaneous Expense)

Petty Cash Voucher
Balloon Adventures

No. 121

Paid To: _John Joseph_

Account: _J. Joseph, Drawing_   Date _July 24, 20--_

For: _Personal use_   _Amount $50.00_

Balloon Adventures
Cash Revenue Report

For Period _July 20-26, 20--_   Date _July 27, 20--_

Income from Tours Credit	Sales Tax Payable Credit	Net Cash Debit
$2,050.00	$168.10	$2,218.10

Balloon Adventures
Memorandum

To _____Bookkeeper_____

From _____J. Joseph_____   Date _July 28, 20--_

Issued check # 1768, in the amount of $184.00, to Castle Security for monthly service charges. (Debit Miscellaneous Expense)

Balloon Adventures
Memorandum

To   _Bookkeeper_

From   _J. Joseph_   Date _July 28, 20--_

Issued check # 1769, in the amount of $22.50, to the Sedona Red Rock News for a 2-line classified ad to run Wednesday and Friday.

Petty Cash Voucher
Balloon Adventures

No. 122

Paid To: _John Joseph_

Account: _Miscellaneous Expense_   Date _July 28, 20--_

For: *Raffle tickets for Corvette for Boys and Girls Club Fund Raiser.*
                              Amount $50.00

Balloon Adventures

Memorandum

To   _Bookkeeper_

From   _J. Joseph_   Date _July 29, 20--_

Poco Javalina Restaurant bought four Balloon Chaser Van Seats @ $50.00 each on account.

Balloon Adventures

Memorandum

To   _Bookkeeper_

From   _J. Joseph_   Date _July 30, 20--_

Issued check # 1770, in the amount of $24.00, for June and July Red Rock Waste Management garbage pickup. (Debit Utilities Expense)

Balloon Adventures
Memorandum

To _____ *Bookkeeper* _____

From _____ *J. Joseph* _____   Date _____ *July 31, 20- -* _____

1. *Compute the payroll below and then complete the payroll register.*

2. *Journalize the payroll and all employee and employer taxes covering period of July 16 to 31—overtime does not apply since nobody has worked more than 40 hours in a week.*

Becky Cedergren (64 hours @ $21.00 per hour), Check # 1771
  Gross amount (hours x rate)
  Federal income tax withheld (Married, 1 deduction) ___196.00___
  Social Security tax withheld (taxable earnings x 0.062)
  Medicare tax withheld (taxable earnings x 0.0145)
  Medical insurance withheld ($40 on first check of month only)
  Net amount (calculate gross amount minus deductions)

Brian Osborn (62 hours @ $19.50 per hour), Check # 1772
  Gross amount (hours x rate)
  Federal income tax withheld (Married, 1 deduction) ___159.00___
  Social Security tax withheld (taxable earnings x 0.062)
  Medicare tax withheld (taxable earnings x 0.0145)
  Medical insurance withheld ($40 on first check of month only)
  Net amount (calculate gross amount minus deductions)

You (56 hours @ $14.50 per hour), Check # 1773
  Gross amount (hours x rate)
  Federal income tax withheld (Married, 2 deductions) ___75.00___
  Social Security tax withheld (taxable earnings x 0.062)
  Medicare tax withheld (taxable earnings x 0.0145)
  Medical insurance withheld ($40 on first check of month only)
  Net amount (calculate gross amount minus deductions)

* Note that the limit on Social Security is $84,900 and that there is no limit on Medicare.

Balloon Adventures
Memorandum

To   _Bookkeeper_

From   _J. Joseph_   Date _July 31, 20--_

1.   Issued checks 1771 through 1773 for payroll period ending July 31, 20--.

2.   Journalize the State Unemployment Tax @ 5.4% of the taxable earnings for this payroll. *

3.   Journalize the Federal Unemployment Tax @ 0.8% of the taxable earnings for this payroll as well as the employer's portion of Federal Unemployment Tax. *

* Note: Federal Unemployment and State Unemployment taxes apply only to the first $7,000 of earnings per year. See the payroll register for earnings taxed up to this payroll.

Balloon Adventures
Memorandum

To   _Bookkeeper_

From   _J. Joseph_   Date _July 31, 20--_

Issued check # 1774, in the amount of $950.00, for my personal use.

Balloon Adventures
Memorandum

To   _Bookkeeper_

From   _J. Joseph_   Date   _July 31, 20- -_

Please total all Petty Cash transactions for the month of July. Then issue check # 1775 to reimburse the Petty Cash box. Verify the amount of $147.18.

Balloon Adventures
Memorandum

To   _Bookkeeper_

From   _J. Joseph_   Date   _July 31, 20- -_

Issued check # 1776 in the amount of $192.05, to State Employment Security for the previous quarter's state unemployment tax.

Balloon Adventures
Memorandum

To   _Bookkeeper_

From   _J. Joseph_   Date _July 31, 20--_

Issued check # 1777, in the amount of $83.20, to City Bank for the previous quarter's federal unemployment tax.

Balloon Adventures
Cash Revenue Report

For Period   _July 27-31, 20--_   Date _July 31, 20--_

Income from Tours Credit	Sales Tax Payable Credit	Net Cash Debit
$2,550.00	$209.10	$2,759.10

Balloon Adventures
Memorandum

To _____Bookkeeper_____

From _____J. Joseph_____   Date _July 31, 20 - -_

Complete the bank reconciliation form and journalize the necessary
entries.

*   _The bank statement balance of cash is $76,235.60._

*   _All checks and deposits were recorded by the bank <u>except those</u>_
      <u>_checks dated July 31._</u>

*   _The bank charge is $12.00._

*   _There was an NSF check from a customer for $58._

Balloon Adventures

Memorandum

To   <u>Bookkeeper</u>

From   <u>J. Joseph</u>   Date   *July 31, 20--*

End-of-the-month work to be completed.

		Version A	Version B
I.	**Prepare the work sheet:**		
1.	Complete the trial balance (preadjusted)	$ 611,007.23	$ 600,260.23
	Ending balance of Cash account	72,185.59	72,185.59
2.	Complete the adjustments columns	2,187.67	2,609.67
	Information for the adjustments is as follows:		
a.	Expired insurance for the month	214.67	214.67
b.	Depreciation of Building for the month	1,220.00	1,440.00
c.	Depreciation of Balloons and Gondolas for the month	320.00	500.00
d.	Depreciation of the Van for the month	218.00	260.00
e.	Depreciation of Office Equipment for the month	130.00	100.00
f.	Depreciation of Balloon Accessories for the month	85.00	95.00
3.	Complete the adjusted trial balance	612,980.23	602,655.23
4.	Extend totals to the income statement and balance sheet columns.		
5.	Compute column totals and net income	Net Income	Net Loss
		400.85	21.15

			Version A	Version B
II.	**Prepare financial statements:**			
A.	Income Statement for Month Ended July 31, 20--			
B.	Statement of Owner's Equity for Month Ended July 31, 20--		313,009.55	301,642.55
C.	Balance Sheet for July 31, 20--.			
	Total Assets		590,061.70	578,722.70

		Version A	Version B
IV.	**Journalize and post the adjusting entries.**		
V.	**Journalize and post the closing entries.**		
VI.	**Prepare a post-closing trial balance**	598,781.08	588,034.08

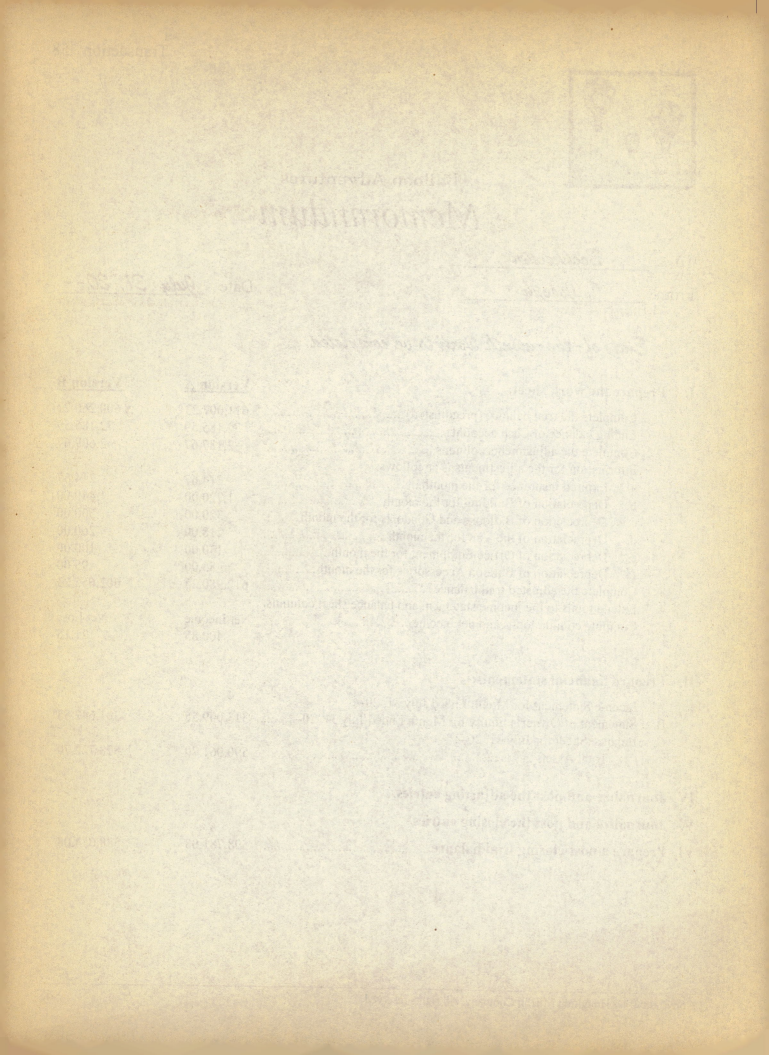

Journals, Registers,
Working Papers,
Report Forms

Balloon Adventures Versions A and B

GENERAL JOURNAL

	DATE	DESCRIPTION	POST. REF.	DEBIT	CREDIT	
1	20--					1
2						2
3						3
4						4
5						5
6						6
7						7
8						8
9						9
10						10
11						11
12						12
13						13
14						14
15						15
16						16
17						17
18						18
19						19
20						20
21						21
22						22
23						23
24						24
25						25
26						26
27						27
28						28
29						29
30						30
31						31
32						32
33						33
34						34
35						35
36						36
37						37
38						38
39						39
40						40
41						41
42						42
43						43
44						44
45						45

GENERAL JOURNAL

	DATE	DESCRIPTION	POST. REF.	DEBIT	CREDIT	
1	20--					1
2						2
3						3
4						4
5						5
6						6
7						7
8						8
9						9
10						10
11						11
12						12
13						13
14						14
15						15
16						16
17						17
18						18
19						19
20						20
21						21
22						22
23						23
24						24
25						25
26						26
27						27
28						28
29						29
30						30
31						31
32						32
33						33
34						34
35						35
36						36
37						37
38						38
39						39
40						40
41						41
42						42
43						43
44						44
45						45

GENERAL JOURNAL

PAGE ___118___

	DATE	DESCRIPTION	POST. REF.	DEBIT	CREDIT	
1	20--					1
2						2
3						3
4						4
5						5
6						6
7						7
8						8
9						9
10						10
11						11
12						12
13						13
14						14
15						15
16						16
17						17
18						18
19						19
20						20
21						21
22						22
23						23
24						24
25						25
26						26
27						27
28						28
29						29
30						30
31						31
32						32
33						33
34						34
35						35
36						36
37						37
38						38
39						39
40						40
41						41
42						42
43						43
44						44
45						45

GENERAL JOURNAL

	DATE	DESCRIPTION	POST. REF.	DEBIT	CREDIT	
1	20--					1
2						2
3						3
4						4
5						5
6						6
7						7
8						8
9						9
10						10
11						11
12						12
13						13
14						14
15						15
16						16
17						17
18						18
19						19
20						20
21						21
22						22
23						23
24						24
25						25
26						26
27						27
28						28
29						29
30						30
31						31
32						32
33						33
34						34
35						35
36						36
37						37
38						38
39						39
40						40
41						41
42						42
43						43
44						44
45						45

Balloon Adventures Versions A and B

GENERAL JOURNAL

	DATE		DESCRIPTION	POST. REF.	DEBIT	CREDIT	
1	20--						1
2							2
3							3
4							4
5							5
6							6
7							7
8							8
9							9
10							10
11							11
12							12
13							13
14							14
15							15
16							16
17							17
18							18
19							19
20							20
21							21
22							22
23							23
24							24
25							25
26							26
27							27
28							28
29							29
30							30
31							31
32							32
33							33
34							34
35							35
36							36
37							37
38							38
39							39
40							40
41							41
42							42
43							43
44							44
45							45

GENERAL JOURNAL

	DATE		DESCRIPTION	POST. REF.	DEBIT	CREDIT	
1	20--						1
2							2
3							3
4							4
5							5
6							6
7							7
8							8
9							9
10							10
11							11
12							12
13							13
14							14
15							15
16							16
17							17
18							18
19							19
20							20
21							21
22							22
23							23
24							24
25							25
26							26
27							27
28							28
29							29
30							30
31							31
32							32
33							33
34							34
35							35
36							36
37							37
38							38
39							39
40							40
41							41
42							42
43							43
44							44
45							45

GENERAL JOURNAL   PAGE ____122____

	DATE		DESCRIPTION	POST. REF.	DEBIT	CREDIT	
1	20--						1
2							2
3							3
4							4
5							5
6							6
7							7
8							8
9							9
10							10
11							11
12							12
13							13
14							14
15							15
16							16
17							17
18							18
19							19
20							20
21							21
22							22
23							23
24							24
25							25
26							26
27							27
28							28
29							29
30							30
31							31
32							32
33							33
34							34
35							35
36							36
37							37
38							38
39							39
40							40
41							41
42							42
43							43
44							44
45							45

GENERAL JOURNAL

	DATE		DESCRIPTION	POST. REF.	DEBIT	CREDIT	
1	20--						1
2							2
3							3
4							4
5							5
6							6
7							7
8							8
9							9
10							10
11							11
12							12
13							13
14							14
15							15
16							16
17							17
18							18
19							19
20							20
21							21
22							22
23							23
24							24
25							25
26							26
27							27
28							28
29							29
30							30
31							31
32							32
33							33
34							34
35							35
36							36
37							37
38							38
39							39
40							40
41							41
42							42
43							43
44							44
45							45

GENERAL JOURNAL

	DATE	DESCRIPTION	POST. REF.	DEBIT	CREDIT	
1	20--					1
2						2
3						3
4						4
5						5
6						6
7						7
8						8
9						9
10						10
11						11
12						12
13						13
14						14
15						15
16						16
17						17
18						18
19						19
20						20
21						21
22						22
23						23
24						24
25						25
26						26
27						27
28						28
29						29
30						30
31						31
32						32
33						33
34						34
35						35
36						36
37						37
38						38
39						39
40						40
41						41
42						42
43						43
44						44
45						45

Balloon Adventures Versions A and B

GENERAL JOURNAL

PAGE _____ 125

	DATE		DESCRIPTION	POST. REF.	DEBIT	CREDIT	
1	20--						1
2							2
3							3
4							4
5							5
6							6
7							7
8							8
9							9
10							10
11							11
12							12
13							13
14							14
15							15
16							16
17							17
18							18
19							19
20							20
21							21
22							22
23							23
24							24
25							25
26							26
27							27
28							28
29							29
30							30
31							31
32							32
33							33
34							34
35							35
36							36
37							37
38							38
39							39
40							40
41							41
42							42
43							43
44							44
45							45

Balloon Adventures Versions A and B

GENERAL LEDGER

Account: Cash   Account No.   111

DATE	ITEM	POST. REF.	DEBIT	CREDIT	BALANCE	
					DEBIT	CREDIT
20--						

GENERAL LEDGER

Account: Change Fund

Account No.   112

DATE	ITEM	POST. REF.	DEBIT	CREDIT	BALANCE	
					DEBIT	CREDIT
20--						

Account: Petty Cash Fund

Account No.   113

DATE	ITEM	POST. REF.	DEBIT	CREDIT	BALANCE	
					DEBIT	CREDIT
20--						

Account: Accounts Receivable

Account No.   114

DATE	ITEM	POST. REF.	DEBIT	CREDIT	BALANCE	
					DEBIT	CREDIT
20--						

Account: Prepaid Insurance

Account No.   115

DATE	ITEM	POST. REF.	DEBIT	CREDIT	BALANCE	
					DEBIT	CREDIT
20--						

Account: Land

Account No.   120

DATE	ITEM	POST. REF.	DEBIT	CREDIT	BALANCE	
					DEBIT	CREDIT
20--						

Balloon Adventures Versions A and B

GENERAL LEDGER

Account: Building   Account No.   121

DATE	ITEM	POST. REF.	DEBIT	CREDIT	BALANCE DEBIT	BALANCE CREDIT
20--						

Account: Accumulated Depreciation, Building   Account No.   122

DATE	ITEM	POST. REF.	DEBIT	CREDIT	BALANCE DEBIT	BALANCE CREDIT
20--						

Account: Balloons and Gondolas   Account No.   123

DATE	ITEM	POST. REF.	DEBIT	CREDIT	BALANCE DEBIT	BALANCE CREDIT
20--						

Account: Accumulated Depreciation, Balloons and Gondolas   Account No.   124

DATE	ITEM	POST. REF.	DEBIT	CREDIT	BALANCE DEBIT	BALANCE CREDIT
20--						

Account: Van   Account No.   125

DATE	ITEM	POST. REF.	DEBIT	CREDIT	BALANCE DEBIT	BALANCE CREDIT
20--						

Account: Accumulated Depreciation, Van   Account No.   126

DATE	ITEM	POST. REF.	DEBIT	CREDIT	BALANCE DEBIT	BALANCE CREDIT
20--						

GENERAL LEDGER

Account: Office Equipment   Account No.   127

DATE	ITEM	POST. REF.	DEBIT	CREDIT	BALANCE	
					DEBIT	CREDIT
20--						

Account: Accumulated Depreciation, Office Equipment   Account No.   128

DATE	ITEM	POST. REF.	DEBIT	CREDIT	BALANCE	
					DEBIT	CREDIT
20--						

Account: Balloon Accessories   Account No.   129

DATE	ITEM	POST. REF.	DEBIT	CREDIT	BALANCE	
					DEBIT	CREDIT
20--						

Account: Accumulated Depreciation, Balloon Accessories   Account No.   130

DATE	ITEM	POST. REF.	DEBIT	CREDIT	BALANCE	
					DEBIT	CREDIT
20--						

Balloon Adventures Versions A and B

GENERAL LEDGER

Account: Accounts Payable   Account No.   211   *

DATE	ITEM	POST. REF.	DEBIT	CREDIT	BALANCE DEBIT	CREDIT
20--						

Account: Sales Tax Payable   Account No.   212

DATE	ITEM	POST. REF.	DEBIT	CREDIT	BALANCE DEBIT	CREDIT
20--						

Account: Employees' Income Tax Payable   Account No.   213

DATE	ITEM	POST. REF.	DEBIT	CREDIT	BALANCE DEBIT	CREDIT
20--						

Balloon Adventures Versions A and B

GENERAL LEDGER

Account: FICA Tax Payable   Account No.   214

DATE	ITEM	POST. REF.	DEBIT	CREDIT	BALANCE DEBIT	CREDIT
20--						

Account: Employees' Medical Insurance Payable   Account No.   215

DATE	ITEM	POST. REF.	DEBIT	CREDIT	BALANCE DEBIT	CREDIT
20--						

Account: State Unemployment Tax Payable   Account No.   216

DATE	ITEM	POST. REF.	DEBIT	CREDIT	BALANCE DEBIT	CREDIT
20--						

Account: Federal Unemployment Tax Payable   Account No.   217

DATE	ITEM	POST. REF.	DEBIT	CREDIT	BALANCE DEBIT	CREDIT
20--						

Balloon Adventures Versions A and B

GENERAL LEDGER

Account: Wages Payable   Account No.   218

DATE	ITEM	POST. REF.	DEBIT	CREDIT	BALANCE	
					DEBIT	CREDIT
20--						

Account: Mortgage Payable   Account No.   220

DATE	ITEM	POST. REF.	DEBIT	CREDIT	BALANCE	
					DEBIT	CREDIT
20--						

GENERAL LEDGER

Account: J. Joseph, Capital   Account No.   311

DATE	ITEM	POST. REF.	DEBIT	CREDIT	BALANCE DEBIT	CREDIT
20--						

Account: J. Joseph, Drawing   Account No.   312

DATE	ITEM	POST. REF.	DEBIT	CREDIT	BALANCE DEBIT	CREDIT
20--						

Account: Income Summary   Account No.   313

DATE	ITEM	POST. REF.	DEBIT	CREDIT	BALANCE DEBIT	CREDIT
20--						

Account: Income from Tours   Account No.   411

DATE	ITEM	POST. REF.	DEBIT	CREDIT	BALANCE DEBIT	CREDIT
20--						

GENERAL LEDGER

Account: Wages Expense   Account No.   511

DATE	ITEM	POST. REF.	DEBIT	CREDIT	BALANCE DEBIT	BALANCE CREDIT
20--						

Account: Payroll Tax Expense   Account No.   512

DATE	ITEM	POST. REF.	DEBIT	CREDIT	BALANCE DEBIT	BALANCE CREDIT
20--						

Account: Advertising Expense   Account No.   513

DATE	ITEM	POST. REF.	DEBIT	CREDIT	BALANCE DEBIT	BALANCE CREDIT
20--						

Account: Fuel Expense   Account No.   514

DATE	ITEM	POST. REF.	DEBIT	CREDIT	BALANCE DEBIT	BALANCE CREDIT
20--						

Account: Utilities Expense   Account No.   515

DATE	ITEM	POST. REF.	DEBIT	CREDIT	BALANCE DEBIT	BALANCE CREDIT
20--						

Balloon Adventures Versions A and B

GENERAL LEDGER

Account: Balloon Supplies Expense   Account No.   516

DATE	ITEM	POST. REF.	DEBIT	CREDIT	BALANCE	
					DEBIT	CREDIT
20--						

Account: Office Supplies Expense   Account No.   517

DATE	ITEM	POST. REF.	DEBIT	CREDIT	BALANCE	
					DEBIT	CREDIT
20--						

Account: Insurance Expense   Account No.   518

DATE	ITEM	POST. REF.	DEBIT	CREDIT	BALANCE	
					DEBIT	CREDIT
20--						

Account: Balloon Repair Expense   Account No.   519

DATE	ITEM	POST. REF.	DEBIT	CREDIT	BALANCE	
					DEBIT	CREDIT
20--						

Account: Depreciation Expense, Building   Account No.   520

DATE	ITEM	POST. REF.	DEBIT	CREDIT	BALANCE	
					DEBIT	CREDIT
20--						

Account: Depreciation Expense, Balloons and Gondolas   Account No.   521

DATE	ITEM	POST. REF.	DEBIT	CREDIT	BALANCE	
					DEBIT	CREDIT
20--						

Balloon Adventures Versions A and B

GENERAL LEDGER

Account: Depreciation Expense, Van   Account No.   522

DATE	ITEM	POST. REF.	DEBIT	CREDIT	BALANCE	
					DEBIT	CREDIT
20--						

Account: Depreciation Expense, Office Equipment   Account No.   523

DATE	ITEM	POST. REF.	DEBIT	CREDIT	BALANCE	
					DEBIT	CREDIT
20--						

Account: Depreciation Expense, Balloon Accessories   Account No.   524

DATE	ITEM	POST. REF.	DEBIT	CREDIT	BALANCE	
					DEBIT	CREDIT
20--						

Account: Interest Expense   Account No.   525

DATE	ITEM	POST. REF.	DEBIT	CREDIT	BALANCE	
					DEBIT	CREDIT
20--						

Account: Miscellaneous Expense   Account No.   526

DATE	ITEM	POST. REF.	DEBIT	CREDIT	BALANCE	
					DEBIT	CREDIT
20--						

CHECK AND DEPOSIT REGISTER					
DATE	CHECK NO.	PAYEE or MAKER	AMT. OF CHECK (Decrease)	AMT. OF DEPOSIT (Increase)	BALANCE OF CASH
20--					65,340.00

PETTY CASH PAYMENTS RECORD

Period of Time: _____   PAGE _____ 30 _____

DATE	VOUCHER NUMBER	EXPLANATION	PAYMENTS	OFFICE SUPPLIES EXPENSE	BALLOON SUPPLIES EXPENSE	J. JOSEPH, DRAWING	MISC. EXPENSE
20--							
	119						

Balloon Adventures Versions A and B

Payroll Register for the Two-Week Period Ending _____ July 15, 20-- _____

	NAME	HOURS	BEGINNING CUMULATIVE EARNINGS	EARNINGS	ENDING CUMULATIVE EARNINGS	TAXABLE EARNINGS		
						UNEMPLOY-MENT	SOCIAL SECURITY	MEDICARE
1	Cedegren, Becky		11,340.07					
2	Osborn, Brian		10,706.02					
3			—					
4			22,046.09					
5								
6								
7								

PAGE _____ 96 _____

DEDUCTIONS					PAYMENTS		
FEDERAL INCOME TAX	SOCIAL SECURITY TAX	MEDICARE TAX	MEDICAL INSURANCE	TOTAL	NET AMOUNT	CK. NO.	
							1
							2
							3
							4
							5
							6
							7

Balloon Adventures Versions A and B

Payroll Register for the Two-Week Period Ending _____ July 31, 20-- _____

| | NAME | HOURS | BEGINNING CUMULATIVE EARNINGS | EARNINGS | ENDING CUMULATIVE EARNINGS | TAXABLE EARNINGS | | |
						UNEMPLOY-MENT	SOCIAL SECURITY	MEDICARE
1	Cedegren, Becky							
2	Osborn, Brian							
3								
4								
5								
6								
7								

PAGE _____ 97 _____

| DEDUCTIONS | | | | | PAYMENTS | | |
FEDERAL INCOME TAX	SOCIAL SECURITY TAX	MEDICARE TAX	MEDICAL INSURANCE	TOTAL	NET AMOUNT	CK. NO.	
							1
							2
							3
							4
							5
							6
							7

93

Balloon Adventures Versions A and B

Balloon Adventures
Work Sheet
For Month Ended July 31, 20--

	ACCOUNT NAME	TRIAL BALANCE		ADJUSTMENTS	
		DEBIT	CREDIT	DEBIT	CREDIT
1	Cash				
2	Change Fund				
3	Petty Cash Fund				
4	Accounts Receivable				
5	Prepaid Insurance				
6	Land				
7	Building				
8	Accumulated Depreciation, Building				
9	Balloons and Gondolas				
10	Accumulated Depreciation, Balloons and Gondolas				
11	Van				
12	Accumulated Depreciation, Van				
13	Office Equipment				
14	Accumulated Depreciation, Office Equipment				
15	Balloon Accessories				
16	Accumulated Depreciation, Balloon Accessories				
17	Accounts Payable				
18	Sales Tax Payable				
19	Employees' Income Tax Payable				
20	FICA Tax Payable				
21	Employees' Medical Insurance Payable				
22	State Unemployment Tax Payable				
23	Federal Unemployment Tax Payable				
24	Wages Payable				
25	Mortgage Payable				
26	J. Joseph, Capital				
27	J. Joseph, Drawing				
28	Income Summary				
29	Income from Tours				
30	Wages Expense				
31	Payroll Tax Expense				
32	Advertising Expense				
33	Fuel Expense				
34	Utilities Expense				
35	Balloon Supplies Expense				
36	Office Supplies Expense				
37	Insurance Expense				
38	Balloon Repair Expense				
39	Depreciation Expense, Building				
40	Depreciation Expense, Balloons and Gondolas				
41	Depreciation Expense, Van				
42	Depreciation Expense, Office Equipment				
43	Depreciation Expense, Balloon Accessories				
44	Interest Expense				
45	Miscellaneous Expense				
46					
47					
48					
49					

ADJUSTED TRIAL BALANCE		INCOME STATEMENT		BALANCE SHEET		
DEBIT	CREDIT	DEBIT	CREDIT	DEBIT	CREDIT	
						1
						2
						3
						4
						5
						6
						7
						8
						9
						10
						11
						12
						13
						14
						15
						16
						17
						18
						19
						20
						21
						22
						23
						24
						25
						26
						27
						28
						29
						30
						31
						32
						33
						34
						35
						36
						37
						38
						39
						40
						41
						42
						43
						44
						45
						46
						47
						48
						49

Balloon Adventures Versions A and B

Balloon Adventures
Income Statement
For Month Ended July 31, 20--

Revenue:				
Income from Tours				
Expenses:				
Wages Expense				
Payroll Tax Expense				
Advertising Expense				
Fuel Expense				
Utilities Expense				
Balloon Supplies Expense				
Office Supplies Expense				
Insurance Expense				
Balloon Repair Expense				
Depreciation Expense, Building				
Depreciation Expense, Balloons and Gondolas				
Depreciation Expense, Van				
Depreciation Expense, Office Equipment				
Depreciation Expense, Balloon Accessories				
Interest Expense				
Miscellaneous Expense				
Total Expenses				
Net Income/Net Loss				

Balloon Adventures
Statement of Owner's Equity
For Month Ended July 31, 20--

J. Joseph, Capital, July 1, 20--			
Net Income/Loss for July			
Less Withdrawals for July			
Increase/Decrease in Capital			
J. Joseph, Capital, July 31, 20--			

Balloon Adventures
Balance Sheet
July 31, 20--

ASSETS				
Cash				
Change Fund				
Petty Cash Fund				
Accounts Receivable				
Prepaid Insurance				
Land				
Building				
Less Accumulated Depreciation				
Balloons and Gondolas				
Less Accumulated Depreciation				
Van				
Less Accumulated Depreciation				
Office Equipment				
Less Accumulated Depreciation				
Balloon Accessories				
Less Accumulated Depreciation				
Total Assets				
LIABILITIES				
Accounts Payable				
Sales Tax Payable				
Employees' Income Tax Payable				
FICA Tax Payable				
Employees' Medical Insurance Payable				
State Unemployment Tax Payable				
Federal Unemployment Tax Payable				
Wages Payable				
Mortgage Payable				
Total Liabilities				
OWNER'S EQUITY				
J. Joseph, Capital				
Total Liabilities and Owner's Equity				

Balloon Adventures
Post-Closing Trial Balance
July 31, 20--

ACCOUNT NAME	DEBIT	CREDIT
Cash		
Change Fund		
Petty Cash Fund		
Accounts Receivable		
Prepaid Insurance		
Land		
Building		
Accumulated Depreciation, Building		
Balloons and Gondolas		
Accumulated Depreciation, Balloons and Gondolas		
Van		
Accumulated Depreciation, Van		
Office Equipment		
Accumulated Depreciation, Office Equipment		
Balloon Accessories		
Accumulated Depreciation, Balloon Accessories		
Accounts Payable		
Sales Tax Payable		
Employees' Income Tax Payable		
FICA Tax Payable		
Employees' Medical Insurance Payable		
State Unemployment Tax Payable		
Federal Unemployment Tax Payable		
Wages Payable		
Mortgage Payable		
J. Joseph, Capital		

Balloon Adventures
Bank Reconciliation
July 31, 20--

Bank Statement Balance $ _____

Add: Deposits in Transit $ _____

_____ _____

_____ _____

_____ _____

_____ _____ $ _____

Deduct: Outstanding Checks $ _____

_____ _____

_____ _____

_____ _____

_____ _____

_____ _____

_____ _____

Adjusted Bank Statement Balance $ _____

Ledger Balance of Cash $ _____

Add: Interest Income $ _____

_____ _____

_____ _____

_____ _____ $ _____

Deduct: Bank Service Charge $ _____

_____ _____

_____ _____

_____ _____

Adjusted Ledger Balance of Cash $ _____